WE ARE LIVING IN LATE CATAPULTISM.

NOTHING ANSWERS TO THAT
UNCANNINESS EXCEPT
MORE UNCANNI-
NESS
"MOVEMENT, ACTION, GESTURE
AND SOLIDIFIED EPHEMERA."

AHSAHTA PRESS
BOISE, IDAHO

2017

THE NEW SERIES
#78

DAYS AND WORKS

RACHEL BLAU DuPLESSIS

Ahsahta Press, Boise State University, Boise, Idaho 83725-1525
Cover design by Quemadura
Book design by Janet Holmes
ahsahtapress.org

LIBRARY OF CONGRESS CATALOGING-IN-PUBLICATION DATA

Names: DuPlessis, Rachel Blau, author.
Title: Days and works / Rachel Blau DuPlessis.
Description: Boise, Idaho : Ahsahta Press, 2016. | Series: The New Series;
    #78 | Includes bibliographical references.
Identifiers: LCCN 2016047222| ISBN 9781934103722 (softcover) | ISBN
    1934103721 (softcover)
Classification: LCC PS3554.U566 A6 2016 | DDC 818/.54--dc23
LC record available at https://lccn.loc.gov/2016047222

ACKNOWLEDGMENTS

This work was completed in a month during early spring 2014 spent at the Resident
Artists Program of the Djerassi Foundation, Woodside, California. With many thanks for
that opportunity and its gift of time—and place.

Ten sections of this work were published in *Conjunctions 63*: *Speaking Volumes* in Fall
2014. With many thanks to editor Bradford Morrow.

With much respect and many thanks to Janet Holmes and Ahsahta Press.

There are so many things to say at one time and this is one of them. Beginning and ending in writing anything is always a trouble of its own and it is a great trouble to any one doing any writing. That is where the newspaper is interesting, there is really of course no beginning and no ending to anything they are doing, it is when it is and in being when it is being there is no beginning and no ending.

That is because it exists any of every day and any of every day is not mixed up with beginning and ending.

> Gertrude Stein,
> "Narration." *Four Lectures.*

. . . Such things
happening on the side.
What is realism
made of?

> Rachel Blau DuPlessis
> "Writing." *Tabula Rosa.*

Was life created in the deep hot jets of undersea minerals or in the
delivery of left-handed amino acids from outer space? Or. . . ?

Never mind. Once here it
"opened with two quadruple salchows, the first in combination with a
double toe loop, and did seven other triples."

The neutrinos arrived on
Earth before light, because they
could escape from a dying star
unhindered. Photons, or light,
can be pulled into the gravitation-
al sink of a black hole. Not the
neutrino.
"Neutrinos are special because
they can — and mostly do —
pass through just about any-
thing," said Goldberg. "It's not
just that they've traveled so far
to reach us. It's that they're so
different than almost anything
else that we've been able to de-
tect after making the same trip."

There were 5 kinds of sex

small medium large

up down middle

in over out

dibble dabble

warp woof

And much nutrition, in one end and out the other,
which other end is another creature's beginning.
Coming from time, webbed further in time,
things get burned, torn, used up,
wrangled, in an attempt at
                    sustained
                    resonance.

Swamp walk by the ocean,

swamp azalea, boggy brown water.

Gold finch, a dark beret slung down, insolent aviator,

then the mocking bird said "bob white" twice.

Brown shrub-speckled dunes,

and an open smudge of mist

through which the hawk suddenly plunges.

Think of the intense narcissism of the dead,

how they follow and demand—

me, me! me, me! Some are also

going—it! note it! but to get

our attention, given their blankness,

they start where we are.

Blur cannot describe what—but it is all there,

luminous, bumped out, or in shadow,

deep as an almost empty box.

Pentacoast.

Accept the desire to puncture the page, maybe with the penetrating awl created by a Capital "I," with its specific pinhole or pin-hold of light. There would be nothing to say if we did not have these languages with their imperfect pile of pronouns. Creation and boson pulse would surge and furl, but who would know, who would care, who would ask, who would interpret or delight?

A monument to any day
where nothing particularly "happens."
That's the way it is.
But it's all in how the nothing
gets told,

The tilling and toiling.

The toll.

"It's the perfect situation of factors," he said, "that came together to make a real big mess for us."

The days go slow and fast. I'm totally out of phase. Don't sleep at night, don't work the day—just rocketing around in flesh. It's still raining. Or it's still snowing. Or it's unseasonably sunny. In drought. Unequal distribution being a problem.

How can so many things occupy the same space?

"Audio Combine for laptop, toy chimes, music box, ukulele and hand drum." "African grey parrot, blue parrotlet, muted violin, trumpet, stone/bowl of water, Buchia synthesizer, and digital recording." "Mobile phones, coins, foil gum wrappers, keys, heavy jewelry, belt buckles, hair clips, and metal in clothing including buttons, snaps, and underwire bras can set off the detector, so think before you get dressed." This named the large and small. It named inexpressible vibration. It named erasure and coping and performed that. It named everyday sounds and their dispersion, materials and their uses. Is this a scrapbook?

> "Mostly, people allow their trees and shrubs to grow too big, and because of that, when they get encrusted with snow and ice, they break, and then you have the domino effect," Crecraft said. "All you need is one to break, and stuff comes down, and breaks stuff below it."
> Birches, white pines, Bradford pears, and arborvitae are the trees most likely to cause problems during storms, Crecraft said. There have been so many downed trees, he said, that he as not had the opportunity to et to some of the bigger ones.

I was driving the wrong car, for some reason got stopped by the police, had to look for car documents, found only multiple old wallets and worn-out purses no matter where, the glove compartment, the well between the front seats, and I did search everywhere—but no registration, no identification, no license. Fed up by this intensifying failure to find what I needed, I was compelled to wake. I've got to get out of this year, and seal it by putting a swathe of clay over the pages, slip, glaze and irregularity. I need to start a new year now. The date is wrong, but I am ready.

So what if I am having an aesthetic crisis. Who cares? The *doppelgänger* used to be a very popular idea of how to feel. "The progressive" has devolved, in my time, from the desire for (illusion of) imminent revolution to the struggle simply for memory. That happened in forty-five years (plus or minus) of my simple single life. Can you imagine how that feels? I didn't think so. Right now, 2014, life has an odd tense peacefulness. Does it? That is what's called "privilege." "The borderline between a pile of refuse and an artwork was never more than obscure."

We are living in late catapultism.

Nothing answers to that

uncanniness except

more uncanni-

ness

"We went out to check Madoff's auditors, Friehling & Horowitz," Brenner said, referring to a small company in Rockland County, N.Y. "It was a two-man shop in a mall. One of the accountants [David Friehling] spent most of his day at the gym. There was no staff for a $65 billion hedge fund? I told [a prospective Madoff investor] it was stupid to invest."
The client ended up investing anyway, and losing millions of dollars, Brenner said.

"movement, action, gesture and solidified ephemera."

"If you suffer from depression, Jefferson is conducting an important study." That was a biscuit conditional. Someone stole my camera! This was an obvious or easily readable outcry in the dream. Whose room? Then it was proven again, but I cannot remember what the aesthetic crisis was. Stodginess? Immobility? How actually to map and indicate the vectors? The simultaneity of conjunctures as an impossible flood? Maybe you can imagine it. "If that's a telemarketer, I'm not here." Spooked by the entrance of these possibilities and their varying potential outcomes, haunted by the yearning for cross-lights, for extra space, for a different page, things destabilize. Is it as simple as a little red wagon painted blue? When someone said, "you really see around corners," I was flattered for a moment, but knew in fact I didn't see that far. For the world is a furnace, the world is a flood, the world is parched, and I sit quietly as if writing postcards. Judging from the little dishes found in tombs, the dead will need to eat, but must not eat too much.

We will not let them. And then, almost as hungry as they are, "we spin around in the night and are consumed by fire."

Before I departed, I dreamed my dead friend embraced me.
We needed a journey. The experience of pivoting.
We entered the hilly sparkle mindfully, not being sure of the way.

Bright, clear light, filled with sea refraction.
And the clouds, always long, palpable, scudding.
The magnetic boatiness of the place was levitating.

Rangitoto—finally I see it. A loping rise, over the harbor waters.
One solid volcano, three concentric craters, two visible.
Just think of Tesla! A spark instantaneous across the gap.

Fractured impassable rock piles trail out from the explosion.
Small lichen work the lava, making colonies.
It's persisting through a hot bright broken blackness,

slightly tamed, contraposto, by a path.
A "recent" eruption— counting geologically.
The hike took 5 hours.

Black spots before my eyes.
Lava air holes in reverse.
I was walking into time.

He died, a young and ambitious artist, of a cocaine OD and the related heart attack.

It was a long flight, strong headwinds.

If you read *Standing in Another Man's Grave* in bed, what kind of dreams *do* you expect?

"What am I doing?"
"You're eating sweet things; you're eating sugar. It always happens after a death."

I understand, as if from every angle, the Dante-word that means dazed, dazzled, confused, vertiginous, undone, stunned and awe-struck : smarrito. At the beginning. At the end. And punctually in between.

Sing through the scintillate deeps of sky, pulse mists with huffs and beeps, and bounce sweet booms off a sublimity that's packed so tight and wrapped so round, it shimmers, shakes and sometimes downright laughs with its own vast, unreadable astonishment.

"I can pick up the alphabet!" she said. And, as from an artesian well, the other end of the writing came up.

Starry False Solomon's Seal. True and false forget-me-not.

Every plant that exists has several different names.

Floating heart. Spoon-leaved sundew.

Every shell there is. Slipper limpet. Boat shell.

If it is all like this, "whereof one cannot speak" is uneven.

Further, "thereof one must be silent" is milky pure desire.

Last night there was a mist so thick it seemed to smoke the moon.

Tonight the full moon sucked things back so far that

little lives in tidal flats

became exposed,

open to our

glittering eyes.

"I like to call it cosmic dawn," Hubble astronomer Jennifer Lotz said at the American Astronomical Society convention in Washington. "It's when the lights are coming on."

It was a time when star formation was ramping up, and it was far more hectic than now.

"Imagine if you went back 500 million years after the Big Bang and looked around in the sky," astronomer Garth Illingworth of the University of California Santa Cruz said. "Galaxies are closer. They're smaller. They're bright blue and they're everywhere. ... They are probably blobby, small, nothing like our Milky Way."

There were probably no metals at this time, no Earths, said Illingworth, who was on the scientific team using Hubble.

"Things look clumpy and kind of weird," Lotz said.

At the moment when the book becomes questionable, possibly obsolete, or at least not alone in the world of inscriptions on something like a page, it appears that I think in nothing but variants of books.

The stele, the monument, the clay tablet, the scroll, the codex, the electronic screen. A flattened surface on which there are socially legible marks.

Though hypertext externalizes the cultural brain, it cannot sort this out without interventions of another brain.

At a time when—as is claimed by some university penny-pinchers—you don't "need" libraries, at a time when digital archives create a potential web of access across worlds, via languages, territories, nationalisms, and holdings (if also potentially privatized, not open source), I am still considering that discrete entity of intervention—the book. Small, contained intentional arrangements, copies put in circulation.

Who would not worry when the precise college president who eliminated a library as unnecessary and put money down on a total electronic "system" was the very college president, so up to her neck in malfeasance and criminality that suicide was the inevitable and accomplished end? This is a true story. It was in the news.

Without the book, we die? And with it, also. That story has no moral for the book. There was no causation, just correlation.

And correlation does not mean causation. But weren't there links? Wasn't that administrator seduced by, even paid by the profiteers in such "systems"?

On the other hand, people and groups have been put to the sword (the flame, the rack, the flail, the bomb) for not seeing one of those books precisely the way some others saw it.

One moral is: do not destroy the book. Do not destroy the person. Do not destroy the reader.

Awake, awake
today! sings
the wood thrush with a silvery sobbing
gurgling warble

first day of hidden nesting tones.
Tomes.

But St. Lucy's Day was not the shortest day of the year. Of course
not. The shortest is not December 13th, the one he commemorated. It's
December 21st. So what's the story about Donne and his poem? It's
that the British were working on the "old calendar" and did not accept
the newer "Papist calendar." (See "burnings at the stake.") Only in the
18th century was there correlation of days. All the dates before that, in
British history, in British literary history, in early colonial history of
what would come to be the U.S.—are all a week or so off. Plus their year
began in March.

In an eclipse, the engulfing reddish color cast from earth is solemn,
slow and even tedious, but only temporary. It fuses every sunset in the
world, flaring from the invisible light that, passing behind earth, makes
the moon go red. After that, everything again quickens into sidereal
normalcy.

I dreamed of fundamentalists cutting off all my hair as a sign of their
power to impose their will upon my head. Well, through most of human
history, blah blah, the female of our species, blah blah. So this was not
a dream. I told the young women that before Griswold v. Connecticut if
you were married, and then Eisenstadt v. Baird if you were single, you
could not get legal contraception. They were incredulous—they could
not even focus on this fact enough to be aghast. These are the ghosts of
near-by pasts.

So where is the texture of actual time in all that? There are stories and
more stories every day; most are composted and gone. To this, it is
difficult to be resigned, but then again, who wants the clutter? Yet who
knows what Dickinsons were lost? Also I have a very bad memory. This
day, today, is such an iron day. In 1941, we'd been at war one week. In
2012, more children died from guns here in this country than from—
from what? Chicken pox? And it takes so long even to write bad poems.
In the dream is a red thread that has to be properly divided. Who has

the measure? "Each cylinder contains enough nerve gas to kill one billion people," the investigatory commission found. This one fact is so frightening that it is ridiculous. Now pile up the other facts.

Artificial sweeteners turn up in rivers, drinking supplies

Canadian researchers think they have found a great way to trace the travels of treated sewage after it is discharged into rivers: Follow the artificial sweeteners.

The scientists found elevated concentrations of four sweeteners — cyclamate, saccharin, sucralose, and acesulfame — in water samples collected along the length of the Grand River in Ontario.

Commonly used in diet drinks, the sweeteners got into the Grand by way of the 30 sewage treatment plants that empty into the river and its tributaries.

The research, published Dec. 11 in the online journal PLOS ONE, adds to a growing body of evidence that people are spiking waterways and their drinking supplies with an array of compounds that pass through not just them, but even advanced treatment systems.

Antidepressants, antibiotics, steroids, and fragrances are among the products that have been detected in surface waters. Some of the contaminants have been found in fish tissue. Some compounds not only get through sewage plants, they also survive purification of drinking supplies and have been measured in trace amounts in municipal tap water.

The researchers made no attempt to gauge the ecological effects of sweetening a river, which they said were largely unknown.

— *L.A. Times*

Speaking from the spot of dust
inside the whirlwind, there was
a book to come,
one just like this.
It tries to answer to what is.

Perhaps a whirlwind book is something
like these papers bound together
as if one,
yet all the pages
are of different sizes, in quiet tints
of cream or beige or white,
and of different weights and textures.
This was a book made entirely of off-cuts.

The poet said he cleaned his desk
of clippings, insistent squibs,
all he had saved for 15 years
and put them on the page.
A test of how much poetry can hold,
precipitate and saturate.
I want not to know
which is margin, which is text,
which is writing, which is gloss.
And I won't.

Here are days and here are works.
Nothing is actually complete.
One might be making argument,
but only to be clear. Be that as it may.
Portuguese has no W and Italian has no K.
They can always borrow. From another book.

And then there is the mode of the reverie.
Then the mode of the rhapsody.
And these are the oldest mountains on earth.

"Please, don't wish people a Happy Yom Kippur; it's not a happy holiday." Misery on clogged highways, cars, fat, cholesterol. Political misery and sense of squalor and shame. Upset at organic life and its pain—and then I have wasted so much of it. A sense of doom, nothing viable enough. Then forgiveness. Then doom. All this in the space of a few seconds. The yearning to untwist tangled threads in the sewing basket. The impossible mending of a broken basket. The yearning for a form that would impact, layer, outcry and reserve nothing. The yearning for doubled talismans to clarify. One thing written over and under another where both can still be seen. Open a door—bright, billowy, freshening. Then there is the clutter. Lintels of clutter. Thresholds blocked. He told us she now has a recurrence of cancer. Dream: someone setting fire to a hayrick. Life as grain and its straw—nourishing, flammable, explosive. Touch where you are, even unto singeing, and make words into talismans, sparks to flame and go to ash within the cool zones of darkness.

The page was shadowed by stars as the light slowly greened, blued and faded to deep gray. Then star by star, the night sky filled up with itself. So I opened the box that I had received. Inside was a beautiful long snake, cobalt blue with turquoise-green diamonds down its back. Brilliant, startling, and it froze me with wonder. In that brief time, it slithered out and down the cellar stairs. I should have slammed the box shut first! Now there it hides among the junk, the books, in the working innards of the house. Pipes. Dust flaking from the concrete. Cold walls and broken furniture. In the shallow dark, it comes and goes as it alone desires. Back and forth, it stalks the several cellar rooms. I wonder whether I should kill it. Even thinking of this option proved almost impossible. Much less doing the task—for I could not tell if this were the task that I was called to do. The only rationale for this desire was fear. Besides, how would it happen; could I really do it? With what tool? How could I manage any part of this attack, such a beauty, exactly my birthstones? And why did I think that killing was the way? Should I try to put it back in the box—luring it to be re-trapped? What would tempt a free snake to come back? These dilemmas were impossible to solve. There was no way to coordinate any capture. What was my role? What was my vocation? There was no outsmarting such a snake.

I am a miniature torus—get that! some shape in unfollowable
dimensions—space this way, space that way, up and down—and
then what? And I have made and marred. There, just there inside the
challenge of framing and telling, of counting and accounting exists the
challenge of time. Like a cloud, might turn to wisps or falling trails.
Might converge to a point on the horizon. To push time past itself
pushes beyond understanding. Be like nothing in front of the question
of stars. Or even within the memory of stars—always fixed and always
turning. And then the skudding, sliding planets. If they were not there,
we would sink in terror. Our backs would break under the burden
of such emptiness. We would know we were not long for this world.
But knowing they are there, even covered over with our own smog,
airlessness, and wells of unseeing, is a small blessing on our struggling
bonds. That people have discussed what lines to imagine between them
and have told the human tales of jealousy and pursuit, of grasping and
letting be, of signs and tokens that make up seasonal stories is some
consolation for enormities of all kinds.

Like everyone in this
chain, Darby didn't know
the identity of his donor.
He knew it was a woman.
"I call my kidney Sarah
Leigh," he said. "Every-
thing is great. She's func-
tioning well. She's peeing
like a racehorse.

A tilt, a modulation, that is all. A title, a modification. These patterned
numbers exist and are strangely moving (01/01/01; 11/ 12/ 13 and the
like), anything to organize time, to throw a human netting over the
splay of atomic splash and furze. They noted that the nerve gases operate
on the central nervous system and observed: 'The victim staggers, falls,
goes into convulsion, vomits, urinates, defecates, and within a short
time dies from the failure of his vital muscular functions." As graphic
as a bureaucrat. One hopes they never saw this happening. Even, let's
say, in tests on pigs. If success makes you sick—is it a good success?
"Previously the Army had suggested that in the event of an accidental
failure on the arsenal property the nerve gases would be dispersed
harmlessly on the ground."

Then in shavasana—that is, in "corpse" posture: a sexual feeling
suffuses me between my eyebrows and through my vagina. Pure vibe of
desirous life. One way or another. You can count on this. Before she died,
her mother wrote little notes and taped them on objects in the house.
Just like mine. Thus the hand of the dead mother still gives to the living
child.

Everything here is double, double lines. He looked at the book I wrote
and then said, unreadably: "It's so short. I expected it to be longer." "It
is when you read it," I tried to say. "Shavua Tov," she writes. It is a new
week. Seven perfect days to come. And then there is another. As the
raptor carried off the nightingale, she of the speckled neck, he chided

her with contempt, contrasting the overwhelming powers of the strong with the thin claims of the feeble, that is, of the makers of song. "I could claw you apart," he said. The bird's response was not recorded in the story. It's hard to get a grip on all the works of days.

Are these identical units of everyday materials? Are they a lexicon? A listing, a relocation? Is form an operation, or a discovery, or a relationship between these and any other thoughts you can think of. There will be 55 sections—and all will be beginnings. There will be 11 multiplied, if you'd like, for even more interesting patterns. There will be (insert your choice of numbers here), based on months in a year, weeks in a day, seconds in a life, years in an hour. Bird flash in the tree. He said, approximately, "form is nothing more than an extension of *context*." Witty as usual. As for me, the problem is the "nothing more."

Pessoas mean persons.

One who is the end

of me

        by sheer project itself,

      watches the brambles of my particular language,

    American English, blown down the road,

as an ecstatic poem.

This is unnerving.

Franklin McCain was one of four freshmen students from North Carolina A&T State University in Greensboro who sat down at the local "whites only" lunch counter on Feb. 1, 1960.

"The best feeling of my life," McCain said in a 2010 interview with the Associated Press, was "sitting on that dumb stool."

"I felt so relieved," he added. "I felt so at peace and so self-accepted at that very moment. Nothing has ever happened to me since then that topped that good feeling of being clean and fully accepted and feeling proud of me."

Cirrus clouds are always composed of ice crystals. Crisscross broken lines weave social eclipses round our world. Deep-sky objects are catalogued as "Messier." It's simply a proper name, yet one that's all too true. When one night, I saw a bolide or fireball tumble from the sky, I almost drove over the scarp to follow it down. To where? There were four springs from the central fountain, flowing water, milk, honey and wine. When the mix is made, they form a kind of blood, maroon and blue-red, nourishing the roots of the world's oldest trees. In the allegory, one always passes through a small door, which has to be a version of the self, perhaps the self without its ego, rolling into the unknown like a cooked egg off the table and into the world, which ends in a cluster of stars.

I see a pink screen laced with mesh capillaries. So this is what holds the eye together!

I've just seen the back of everything.

> What happened next was swift and brutal. The soldiers seized the man and repeatedly stabbed him.
> "He was dead within two minutes," said Peter Bouckaert of the New York-based Human Rights Watch, who observed the killing.
> Bouckaert documented the vio-

An old woman fusses for coins in a metal click change purse. Fingers twisted cannot pick up dimes. The years move along; she lives in her webbings of electricity making small sparks. She picks out a quarter. Eventually she will have nothing in her purse and lack the fine-tuned touch to take the change. O now dead woman, did you feel an erotic dream of writing and of books—a kind of desire identifying the words with the breadth of your rapacious and incommensurate yearning?

The newest dead land story concerns a drained and ruined ecology. The other news story details another bombing—people in pieces. One's frustration, one's resistant disgust with the politics of others (which are also officially one's own), proves what point? What would social good really look like? The shadowy was taking shape. This darkness held the "I" together.

> lence in a series of tweeted photos. The victim's leg was severed.
> "A man just walked up with the severed leg of the lynching victim, just walking around," tweeted a shocked Bouckaert.

And the most suggestive recent typo was allienation.

If we all become radioactive. . . . It's simple. It could happen from the atomic event boring down under the toxic nuclear reactor split to its core by a quake and washed by a tsunami. Whoever thought that was a good idea—but litotes and irony seem misplaced. One urbane twist too many. Note the role of superheroes to naturalize this kind of drastic outcome: we get super powers! Hey, Peter Parker, you are an enormous act of social condensation and *détournement*! Mazel Tov. Now, back in reality: What is the level and nature of emergency? Is it that life goes on parallel tracks—the quotidian and its splendid minutiae (discarding junk mail; scattering salt on an icy walk; mending holes in socks, though not darning them with the little weave my mother formerly did; throwing away the trash someone tossed on the street; cutting up an apple) and the simultaneous sense of disaster? When the minutiae and the disaster cross? With what force—or are they still only parallel, infinitesimally closer together, magnetically inseparable, yet still only parallel lines.

Talk about the future emergency, the recognition of precarious extremities, the still- theoretical moment of decision—stay or go? how far can you get? when and how? whom to trust? Roads are clogged. Money is crucial but almost useless, except it might remove a person from the prevailing winds. People speculate in water; the price rises. They hoard whatever stuff they find. There might be any outcome—one is thrown to the fates of further chance. Perhaps there will be grave vases—a big tube, a vat, open at both ends. One end open under earth, one end open to air and light and rain. The connector tube between realms. I mean, we will light the dead with a faint remembrance, but they also light us with the dark light of respect for the processes we have destabilized and offer some necessary taboo on tampering. We are not the Masters of the Universe; we are the Masters of Unintended Consequences.

What does it mean to "escape"? it means postpone.

Do I mean an ethical art? Has not this experiment already been tried? Can poetry invent a script and begin to speak again of powers and processes? And what should it do—simply contain or solemnify the sense of doom? A poetry of mourning, eternity, and consolation. Or rouse responses?

> She signed and finger-printed a blank piece of paper after officers told her they had detained her teen-age daughter and would rape her. She says her lawyer later told her she was accused of blowing up a house and other attacks.

A poetry of naming, naming, of joining insights by naming, inside the time we live because this is our time. Experiment with the means. Affirm the critique. Never forget that the build comes inside history, inside what we see as now, infused by the works and days that other times have offered. Stand, negotiating understanding, even as you articulate the cosmopolitanism of hope.

Execute
        command 135
        statement 135
Execute SQL
        command 128, 130
        dialog box 128, 130
Executing
        DDE commands 137
        procedures 129–131
        SQL statements 129

What was that shadow from the air? Black matter edged with blue. How could that be only the angle of sun over snow scarps, such "unreality" in reality demands something new about reality. What was I about to say—such an opening: note it, note it.

> The woman was execut-ed seven months after meeting with HRW, in September 2013, despite lower court rulings that dis-missed some of the charg-es because a medical re-port documented she was tortured into confessing.

Sometimes I think things are harder than people make them, and other times I think—well, easier. It's incommensurate. Meaning—I'm not in sync with the questions people pose, with the contexts, with the absolutism or austerity of the questions, or with the get-along norms, to which my answers are often non-ontological banalities (like "just do the best you can without hurting anyone or using up too many things") but at other times terrifyingly ontological absolutisms ("I think the earth itself will not survive—not in the form we know and are used to"). Then I immediately consider—but the earth has never "survived" in the way that this sentence formulates—static, unchanging. Just because we are used to something! Speak of human ego. It is not made for us, though it is, currently, about us. This is the first delusion. And perhaps the second, too. And then I modify—why is it I think all this—is it the scale of the disaster? the useless, scarifying strife, not the productive struggle? the extent and diversity of the multiple damage? a sense of intensity and nearness? a clock actively ticking? a qualitative change of impacts? a dread mapped onto the arc of my life? So how can I talk about it? I mean, precisely, what words and syntaxes can I possibly use, what images and intonations actually will give any feeling-intelligence from this double-sided existence ("do the best you can although the earth is doomed")?

X. is back from China (it's 1989). She said it was mostly "the people"—
regular common folks—who got killed. Because they were in Tiananmen
Square, protecting the students and, actually, just curious. Wanted to
see. The way you would be. X. said, "they lined up the tanks twenty
across and fired into people." government amounts
to a crime against humani-
ty because it is part of a
policy of spreading terror
and mental anguish
among those left wonder-
ing about their loved ones.

I told the child a sanitized version of this news—now not entirely sure
why. She said of the demonstrators, "Why don't they get into their cars
and drive away from the army." She said, "Why don't they just call the
police?"

Of the monarch butterfly chrysalis—these are green and have a set of
the smallest golden dots in a line. When the chrysalis turns clear and
the butterfly collects or forms its readiness, the line of dots becomes
coppery-silver. Should I comment here that the monarchs are now in
gravest danger? Corporate agriculture and its rampant herbicides have
chewed through their terrain, their stands of milkweed, even unto the
smallest uncultivated borders along the sides of roads and fields. If they
cannot eat, they will not live.

How much is enough, how much is too much. When does one's anger
rise to agency? There is no formula for disclosure. If one hesitates
over adequacy, years go by. And there are many goals, simultaneously
unfulfilled. It appears this is the 21st century now. About thirty years
have passed since X.'s trip. And it's exactly one hundred years since the
first World War. The Unnecessary One. But there were always murders,
infiltrations, betrayals, conflicts, loud claims of multiple vanguards,
gurus, dictators, disinformation, bribes, "this war will pay for itself,"
losses of nerve, ginning up to fight, declaring an enemy, ultimate

26

opposites, final battles, conflicted conviction, silent or proud dissent, suicides, and normal life—years go by. How quickly useless misery can occur; how woven into the daily; how transforming.

regime began dropping "barrel bombs" filled with hundreds of pounds of explosives and shrapnel on apartment buildings in their neighborhood, killing hundreds of civilians and wounding hundreds more. The three were planning to rush back into the mayhem.

"There are not enough doctors or nurses or supplies," Asma explained

He has power cords snaking through his work—he never shows the outlets where they're plugged in. The places he depicts in these prints are neither inside nor outside; they are tents and they are huts, temporary encampments, people needing to flee, trash left where they lay down to rest and then decamped to flee some more. The sites he has drawn are empty of people. And those cords—power source vague— must be plugged in to some diesel generator or be stealing from the one measly electrical pole stuck in this neglected banlieu. This literalizes the obfuscation and featureless dispersal of power, we all feel it, moving silently through our landscapes, but coming from where? going where? The noises are off. It is hard to track, although one sees the evidence. As the cords disappear to the side, one gets distracted by the garbage and the jerry-built shelters, torn between saying "this looks so trashy" and "I'm so sorry."

As the number of cupboard clients has increased, the number of people living unsheltered — in cars, the woods, even coin-operated laundries — has grown nearly 100 percent from last year, from 24 to 43 people, Hackman said.

"Grasses for sheep in Australia." Where did this statement come from? Should the sheep have been brought there in the first place? Insofar as life, or writing is continuous, it continues. Insofar as it was interrupted, it is a risk, a cliff, a scarp, a challenge, a fall. "Encyclopedic"?—now implausible. Try instead a symbol of the encyclopedic. That would be what? Consider it. A constant scan of everything—systematically—one sentence about food, one about time, one for clouds—a factual-technical account; one for the window, one for the dream. Then repeat and repeat. This is a form, invented right here (lucky you); this all could be arranged. Consider the outcome and impact, consider the compounding and the combining necessary—yes, of course. Now we don't have to do it. A concept doesn't demand its carry through. That constraint can't tie you down. Good enough, but too systematic for all this.

A symbol of the encyclopedic? Perhaps the alphabet. Whose? Certainly not the one without a K. OK—ours. Anglophone Hegemonic. "Holistic"— now that was one of those words that pulsed forward back in the day as a solution to daily life, a word now evocative of its time. A word both inside and outside, in the air and intestinal, heart-felt. Peristaltic? An ambition to get everything in and then evacuate the question itself, for now all things were fused. (Like an ecosystem left undisturbed. Joke.) Is that in fact the alphabet? Is that a system in which individual parts are intimately connected to the whole? It seems so when we sing its little song. But it is intimately historical and also simply convenient. It does not automatically fit together, no jostling, no clashes. There are other alphabets; they have their little songs. "Holistic": An Edenic reversion to something never was. Plus that false etymology with its touch of "holy." Holistic—interdependent—of course—but in the sense of having no friction, no strife? Now this seems unlikely, and always did.

A symbol of the encyclopedic—mysterious numbers emerging from bubbles and nets of planetary fecundity—from the multi-universe itself: generative and febrile and metamorphic, with "feverish" indicating an entirely different scale of time and size and place than we have ever really seen. An entirely different scale of the meaningful. An unfindable scale, in short, of the meaningful. Should I make art based entirely upon chance? Next question: Using what human system of number or design? Is there any chance within our scale?

So sentences get interrupted, modified, snarled, swamped by phrases, demurrals, reachings irritably, undermining the very statement that stating demanded. Sentences—judicial, yet undone by wayward desires, by undertones of injustice. Then everything came along, or fell bumping down the slope, fractured individually, but used prosthetically. For how to put our "everything" together was the dilemma. Then someone usefully thought to use the cloud beyond the brain to store the collective—but still selective—brain. The brain of the world, indicating its abundance with the numerology of googol, and then, in addition, with its re-spelled brand name.

"Inclusive" was a sweet thought, what with contradictions everywhere, hands reaching against each other for food and clothing, the struggles over access to water, delivery systems kaput or rife with bribes, the civil war, and the peace of threatened war, with the permanent but invisible war, economies that cannot (yet) be de-turned and retooled for social OK-ness away from production for war. I mean precisely "OK-ness." My party of one. Relative OK-ness in the face of the precarious. Please don't ask for chaos as the "obvious" initiator of a newer bolder order. Things have never actually worked that way. Plus there is always some strong man, some power, some cabal, some country inadequately bored by the banal, predictable costs and decadent blood-lettings of war or disinterestedly inane in the face of the starvations of relative peace. Wanting to get something back, a resentment, a glowering back as far as one can trace—remember that territory? How it was taken away a hundred years ago? Well, it's really ours.

For "war" is generally discussed as from an outside—sanitary, swift, pre-emptive, clean (they even thought that WWI would be that way—in 1914, that is); it can be sold that way back home. To us. A tidy part of our tidiness. And we are made to want it. It takes a certain rigidity and tender-heartedness, uneasy doubt, stubborn principle, or even sheer distaste to resist human sacrifice on a mass scale. Cannibalism (I am not recommending it) might have been more honest. Actually—and this is so simple, I can hardly bring myself to say it—I hope that they (that we) have not been permanently undermined. That is, destroyed.

What is the scale I am using?

> The extremes of life are glaring, cupboard volunteers say.
> "West Chester has become a real foodie place, a gourmet dining area," said volunteer Fiona Allison. "Yet poverty around here is wicked. It's a huge inequality that you see here every day."

Who are we, finally? The osmotic skin of an organic (rounded) quasi-polyhedron through which are exchanged languages (vocabulary, grammar, "templates of fixed positions," even grunting and pointing, plus curses, puns, charms, mantras that no one understands but are felt to be traditionally effective, counting and tallying, right up to "borrowed words and fortuitous resemblances" across language groups); the micro-universe of the personally plausible (desk, apple, bowl, child—you know—the usual examples); the unconscious (him with a black beard when it's really sandy, or another, of fucking a generic man with a generic-gigantic erection); the unknown macro-universe (dark matter, particles escaped before there was light); and the micro- (the way the desk seems solid; the way the apple can be digested); plus cunning strategies of thought and grasp. We have wandered all over the earth, trying it out and changing it, changing us, and any other life forms we've encountered. Yet the more words are said about this (or really about anything), the more there is utter mystery.

"Starry lake of sky with glowing arch of brilliance (or whatever)" said the student poet, trying for a fluffy language. When I said perhaps the children could go outside and play in the fresh air, not sit in front of the television, she said, very huffily, "It's not TV. It's cable." I saw the Life of Marinetti made on twelve ceramic plates, done in 1939. A Stations of the Cross of Fascism. She told us that their mother used to peel their father's peach, because he loved peaches but could not bear to touch the fuzzy skin. The moon, what's left of it, sets beyond noon of the next day. The alphabet was once magical-religious, a new secret technology, worth a pilgrimage to investigate. So the children engaged in the tingling stupor of TV. Then some of them get Ritalin. Mean solar time is time measured by the daily motions of a fictitious body called the "mean sun." That was a rugged landscape with young volcanoes. But this one is a rugged landscape with redwoods, sand hills, and washes of fog. After the dream, I wake up tired. Everything being detail and linkages, I am over-saturated. Neither asleep nor awake, forming fractostratus of bad weather or fractocumulus of bad weather or both, a world-large stage, cellular frustration faced with a cleaving ferocity, ecstatic yearning mixed with panic. If one plugs into power and the rush saturates you and explodes within, if one cannot throw a text-filled shard down as a limit, there will be a final obliteration. How close can one get to an engorgement without being swept out to that sea in which one has tried to exist—swim, wade, bathe, float—in a temporary salt balance with the unimaginable? Yet with a little luck and a lot of time, the exegete can be transformed by the practice of exegesis.

"A harmonious accord of ylang-ylang essence from the Comoros.
Damascena rose essence and sambac jasmine absolute" tell the tale   .
of endless luxury or the image of such, beauty, voluptuous intensity,
magnitudes of sexuality, and world-ranging sources. A picture in an
airplane catalogue, flying high.

On the path in front of me was a Diabolo Range Gartersnake. To tell its
proper name, I quickly checked stripes of yellow and red on dark, its
slender pointed self on lists of local snakes.

> What is the political trace of
> this natural object and that glossy shot
> of the feminine, that I can be here
> just here, as such, looking
> at them—
> for both (and more, whatever,
> we should talk about it)
> seem to represent
> uncolonized pleasure
> and this is delusional
> and I know it,
> but Oh! the attractions and
> apparently ungrounded charms
> of the so-called eternal verities!

Dying through the spring, she wants another spring. But first there will be fall. Body on lease. Never quite one's own. Yet one's only boundary. A kind of booty, the treasure box Pandora opened and let it all escape but one. One tiny death, and after all, some people call it "hope." The lease has run out. The tenant evicted, tenaciously standing with her random stuff, out on the street, the rags and papers blowing through the night. Are words the ghosts? I think they are the ghosts of ghosts. And dogs do know some words, or at least some tones. Suppose, yes, the words are ghosts but cast a long, palpable shadow. This shadow is called "things." But wait! I might have got that backwards, wrong. The words themselves have led me astray, and, pitch proud, they thrust themselves to the head of the line and listed themselves first. They put words in my mouth.

This is a cumulus of considerable development where the large cloud in the center has a horizontal, heavily shaded base, above which heaps of white bulge in cauliflower formation. Under this, one watches the ever-transported dead, and waits to see their changes. A waxy remove. A being somewhere else. Brought to the forefront and enveloped in an unreal nothingness right here in the center of the real. Death—one eye closed, one drooping slightly open. With fairy drops of long repressed tears, her water is draining. This work is posthumous work. One sees the present under the dark light of death—icy, windy, bright and hot, pulpy fog, or night. Despite the orange spurt of sunset swooped across the over-ocean's limpid light blue sky, a black mouth, a black month is getting rounder and gaping more open than before. Everything is bruised and hairy. A snoring quickens and slows, ticking off its own doomed count, and this quite informatively. These ghosts are sitting shiva in the interior of my silence. They listen to the long gasps between breathing. Long, long pauses. There develops the tight inertness of (say it this way, no other) nothing.

Can't you take a joke in a dream? is what the dream said to the feminist. Those books on parenting lined up, and I remember saying "I won't need these books any more." Not sure it was all that funny, given my spotty maternality. Silent moments, blanks, filled with the next pulse of love. Live in time, with an uncertain backbeat. Time is a language in which I am only partially fluent. Maybe better than some. I can make a list of what I have to do. An eerie network of the mixage of one's waking selves. Of and of and of. You are the spirit of my mother. "I am the Ghost of Christmas Past." I had to memorize this line and then another. So I said it was so hot I could not breathe (*respirare*), but what I ended up saying was it was so hot I could not vacuum (*aspirare*). By the way, they say "hoover" in England. At least I think that's what I said. I have fallen into the letter and almost drowned for struggling with my tongue against my palate while the power of languages choked me up. I want to go deeper into the word. Or go against the limits of languages, days, clouds, the changeable, and time. Yet the limits are defining and some are absolute. Then the other character said: "Long past?" And all I had to say was, "No, your past. You will arise and go with me, seeing the things you have need to remember." That archaic grammatical turn made it hard for a little girl to remember. I also think I was confusing *past* and *passed*. The only thing worth doing is porous—breathing into the vacuum, taking void as a herald, and transitory mesh as our little lines.

The ill woman says: "It's really getting very something or other." But who would want her to say: "It's getting far worse"? She says: "It's getting more and more involved." She does not name the "it." If she did not exercise periphrastic un-naming, she would not be herself. She says: "The skin is so deteriorated; it's sore; it weeps." Her constant word is "weeps." Well, that's direct enough.

Her once thick hair, all decay, and all unreal, she says. Time, the loss,
the curiosity (why they cannot talk to her; whence came the compromise
of warmth; why holding on and intensified narrowness did not create
close bonds but silent fraying). Sinks into . . . Cannot say what's on her
. . .

We need an implementation plan for these updated directives.
The blanket overstitch
stichomythia
a doomed dialogue with her
the blanket is still here with its re-made binding
the thread pulled distinctive as handwriting
but decoding falls asunder.

Too many dead messages. Too few glossaries.
Crabbed and crabby writing.

The silent stories settle in random piles
of odd goods left over.
Talismans of wonder that this or that
was saved, his pens, for instance.
Things he could not bear to
throw away
were things that she too
could not throw away
are the things I cannot
bring myself
to throw away.
Where and how
can this possibly end?

QUATRAINS

Suddenly I realized that I was set
among the dead. I was a mix of old
and young, sporting a formerly
fashionable jacket. Jackal.

The library (inevitably) is close to closing.
The librarian announces
"this library is almost closing"
and I answer testily "I know."

There was no time to find any book.
The right book wasn't there anyway.
Set is an Egyptian god. So sue me.
Then I drive home, but was it home?

There were warnings about the Elk River's susceptibility to chemicals. A report prepared by West Virginia officials in 2002 in compliance with the Safe Drinking Water Act found that the water system in the Kanawha Valley, the area affected by the spill, had a high susceptibility to potential contamination. The report identified 53 potential contaminants to the water system, all but four of them from commercial or industrial sources. The area is known locally as Chemical Valley.

It's not clear whether anything was done to address the report's recommendations, and state officials said they were unaware of any more recent

Needed: a "place of full permission." The pear tree now is mostly orange gold, like a flutter of jewelry pendants or coins. Bright wind and twisting light. Three years later, it flowered. Then it suddenly died. That inlet looked paved over with fat white yachts. To this I doubt that anarchism is the answer. And I keep forgetting to write about Jupiter! Gorgeously visible, very close to the moon. But every day, it changes where it is. Until the intensity passes, and it slides slowly away. "Bye, see you soonish!" She said, "T. thinks she moves and acts at the speed of light; the rest of us are just renting." That second ensemble had talent, but understands nothing about the meanings and uses of silence. Do you know, according to this patrician activist I met, that the upper classes "never discriminated against ladies"? You bet not! "I won't clean my room—I like it that way!"

studies. The Safe Water Drinking Act does not give any additional authority to states or utilities to reduce or eliminate threats, said Lynn Thorp, of Clean Water Action.

West Virginia American Water and other utilities serving populations of 50,000 or more were required to submit vulnerability assessments to the EPA in 2003. The EPA keeps the assessments secret, and while it analyzed them to

Remaking, remaking, remaking. Three fainting spells in the Commedia, each marking an unanswerable transition, dilemma or crisis. Was it my mother who filched things from the restaurant, and how did that cutlery, a few random things stuck in something like the basket from a dishwasher, become set upon set of museum-quality silver, with mysterious markings known only to scholars of the decorative arts? And why was I now stuck with this silver as my whole family—the living and the dead—scooted off in small red wagons or in shopping carts? Why? You tell me. And why did I have to try and figure things out with the restaurant, price, cost, slippage, extremity, when no one, including myself, had a clue what to do next. Or what had actually happened. Why did she even take the silver? Why was I stuck with it, just this sliver of living time?

Even if we return to the same point, the journey has altered the starting place.

J's father changed the family name; it became very Scottish. The son discovered his Jewishness only on his father's birth certificate after that death. He himself had been harassed as "Jew-Boy," and had shrugged away this schoolyard taunt. Surprise! I asked him what effect this had on his writing. He laughed and said—"it made me not so afraid to lose my identity, my ego."

C. told me that when his father died in England in 1927, a telegram came from his father's brothers. They took it to the Hungarian Embassy. When translated, it read: "Under British law do we inherit anything?"

How could I write about "imagining God," as someone recently asked me to for an anthology in the series *Graven Images*—? I laughed. "God?" (It was the laugh of Rachel, a motif in the uncollected scriptures of the ancient Israelites, the ones no one has yet unsealed from their scroll-shaped clay vessels.)

The examined life is too complicated to live.

"If you obey my voice and keep my Convenient, you shall be a treasured possession out of all the peoples." A pretty good deal, at least for the Chosen. But it does not account for "redundancy." And its persistence—in the brain, among populations, and fundamentally in language—has to mean a lot. If you just want pat packs of information, correct Scripture, and One oneness, then zero redundancy is the goal, of course. Ultimate code blue, final final, no questions asked. We get it. But multiple meanings, slips of the tongue, misunderstandings or misspellings ("my Convenient"?), statements turning into their opposite, elaboration, build-up in rhetoric—one-two and then THREE—there's the excess and fold, the double text, the over-layering inside the real. Redundancy is the third wish, the flight of fancy, the crooning, crone-ing, crowning sound of muchness.

"A research team led by Dr. John Stamatoyannopoulos, University of Washington, has discovered a second code hidden in DNA. This second code contains information that changes how scientists read the instructions contained in DNA and interpret mutations to make sense of health and disease.

"Since the genetic code was deciphered in the 1960s, scientists have assumed that it was used exclusively to write information about proteins. UW scientists were stunned to discover that genomes use the genetic code to write two separate languages. One describes how proteins are made, and the other instructs the cell on how genes are controlled. One language is written on top of the other, which is why the second language remained hidden for so long."

Thus the necessity for exegesis. And the expectation of surprise.

The God of the Covenant was way into drapery, color and texture, into that extra inch of braid on priestly robes, a band alternating golden bells and pomegranates, and into the color of the curtains on His Ark— purple, scarlet, blue. All those details will hide the Hidden with the lavish redundancy of the aesthetic. And all these things—they made this creature more than just Command. More—well, picky. Odd. More duplicitous. More beautiful and more suspect. Quirky and problematic and queerish and moody.

Of course redundancy, excess, gorgeousness, and a second language are not quite the same things. Although there are similarities. Both create the plural. And more and more to come.

His passport photo—with its restless, worried look—had gigantic crackles of glue that had worked through the old photograph, making open spots on the page. It looked like two bullet holes had just missed his head. How not to be haunted?

Setting out, yes, but the journey becomes much more wayward than the traveler had planned, an experience out of range. Turning to verbs means into risk. What was the ordinary diagnosis? Accounts and additions. The sourness of too warm milk. Unheard words—that contained directions also unheard. Soldiering on, somehow there were traces. Even though it was vast. The traveler had one plan, but the journey had another.

Two days later, Sudler was on a gurney, being wheeled back to her room after a test. "Do you have my oxygen tank?" she asked the aide. He replied, "What tank?"

She began to cry. She realized she was breathing on her own.
Nationally, 1,600 people are waiting for lung transplants. In

The thinnest light of the needle settled at the small pool where the birds alight and raise their little throats to swallow. Two universes meet, page to page. Shapes of delicate and fibrous air pass above us. And the hawk clawed the nightingale as they flew along the edge of sky and out of sight.

Look at how the clouds metamorphose. They are the form of the formless, it was said. They escape taxonomy, it was said. But actually there are high clouds, middle clouds, low clouds and clouds with vertical development; definitions and descriptions of the forms of clouds can be observed, then put into words. As when "the hard and 'cauliflower' swellings soon become confused and melt away so that nothing can be seen in the white mass but vertical fibers. This often occurs very rapidly." Clouds become, for us, the silence. For right here we need to record 60 seconds of room silence. The recording needs a certain quiet breathing in this space. The space has a shape. The air has a dimension. Each room, each different set of people, generates a different texture of silence. The time is a plumb line and a network, webbed inside this clump of atoms and water vapor. Slight humming inside the ears. Slight skewing of this breath. Wind not moving. Downdraft of the encounter. Crust of being. Edit the silence into the record. Even if this silence is only our skeuomorph of silence.

COMPLAINTS

Along the way were lumps of amber big as figs. Too beautiful for words.
This is a complaint.

What Nothing does Zero mean?

In notarikon, the letters become a moving target. When you fill each
word's letters up with other words, the topics shift faster than the
alphabet. You can't keep up with them or with yourself. Language
takes over, saying too many things. It is always the wrong idiom; the
unnecessary periphrastic word. Awkwardness rules. There can be no
follow-through of any metaphors. The arguments cannot be consistent.
The text becomes a field of broken arrows. Excess rules.

For instance, in notarikon-ing English, one finds way too many th-'s.
What with *the* and *there* and *them* and *their* and *these* plus *those* and *this*
and *then*. It looks like not enough good words begin with "h" to make
this all worthwhile. Or they are the wrong words and cannot match the
words that start with "t." It's a thorn in one's side. I cannot make it work.

All the poems in the book tried to stand against the book, and yet they
were inside a book— –

how then to critique the merely literary. Again—how hard it is to make
it work.

Destroyed. And disgusted. And destroyed once more. Ripped, remade.
Began in 1979. Began in 1964. Began again in 1983. Began in 1986. Began
without. Destroyed all "my paintings." Destroyed all "my objects."
Destroyed the work by not doing it. Destroyed the work by overdoing
it. Never one thing. No making pretty images. No making reasonable

objects. No rhetorics of elaboration, no consolation, few expected conclusions. Discontent and resentment. Poems? No poems. No books. No nothing.

Can this be both a book, be several books, be no book? Can it open the pages and unbind them beautifully whilst keeping them together, also beautifully?

Can the book keep open while sometimes closing? Who closes it? the reader might. The writer might. Claims of authority might. The book might also wait silently until its moment is ready. Look how I have given agency to the book! But the temporalities are, anyway, multiple, mutable and diverse. The book, it seems, can be both open and closed.

Can there be a book at the same time about nothing and everything, only about words, and only about concepts; about rips of feelings and pressures of historical fate?

Wouldn't you want to say that this is every book?

Every meaningful book?

"Whilst" is British. I'm not, but I like how it sounds.

Writing goes in one direction only, but seeing—can go out in vectors way beyond the frame. This is another unforeseen challenge, to offer the sense of vectors and pulse inside the book without an overload that cannot be read.

How can a book be polysemous and also thesis-bearing? It is an inexplicable mystery of writing. Whenever you feel this double air, just breathe deeply in with open-hearted breath. And exhale deeper still.

Our universe may or may not have an edge. Most people can think only to that edge. If at all. But a book clearly has an edge. This fact helps us think beyond the edge to what may not have one, or be beyond the all, in a multi-verse (in multi-verses) of excessive temporalities and explosive burgeoning.

Books are universes of edges.

Books are edges of the universe.

We still do not understand that particular "the." "The" universe. Probably it is less painful to accept it.

Why do the extremities of language occur so frequently—the claim that words should just be things, the claim that words are only words in and for themselves—color without resonance, or letters without etymology, or phonemes without a past, or marks without sociality, or messages without specific decoders, their necessities and their practices. Remember redundancy? remember nuances of tone? remember the intricacies of syntax and of word placement. And what about the claim that anything can be done with words, the claim that matter can become pure text?

Why? Because it all has to be experienced, tried, essayed, experimented. And done once more again. Generally this kind of science will have no inhumane consequences. But every once in a while, the experiment goes awry—and some demonic slogan allows for broadside lust in slaughter; then some shibboleth or little lisp or glottal stop or mispronounce will mark your unfortunate head with battered blood.

Anything can be done with words, but what makes those things worth doing?

There is a kind of traditional Korean pottery known as buncheong: freedom of design, unusual shapes, and strange surfaces. This is, of course, a poetry of bunching, a kind of text known for freedom of design, unusual shapes and strange surfaces. Which is why I am mentioning it.

Walk the seam
with monitors of dusk.
Words fail. Yet there must be words.
Do not cede that territory.
Despite impossible transitions.
Meaning cannot be rescued from commerce, power, war. It is not rescue that's needed. These uses must be accepted, enveloped, and yet unveiled as such. These are no more real than any other use.

Draw the rope of the poem tighter and tighter around the words. Despite the unfortunate metaphor, such tightness "is the only way to achieve the floating or uncertain nature of things." This is the paradox of strife. Of an open closedness.

Ambiguity and the between—these are what abide. Though they wobble and vibrate continuously, and they might thereby be hard to track. So no sitting in a vaunted mythic hut is possible. In the between, there is no mystique. Only tacking, and a few stops for rest, inside a restlessness that does not cease.

There is nothing terrible about surplus meanings, but there is something odd about too many of them all at once.

"Here" and "there" are words in geography and grammar, not in ethics.

Thereupon a blessing, the metaphor of starry skies pouring down. Poesis is that blessing.

You're holding in your hand the purest bottled water available.

It is prepared with our patented purification process

removing every detectable impurity

and chemical contaminant. The result?

Clean, crisp-tasting water that helps your body

hydrate faster and more completely—

enabling you to realize

your best mental and physical performance.

Arsenic free. Chlorine free. Fluoride free.

BPA free. MTBE free. Chromium 6 free.

Trace pharmaceuticals free.

Purified drinking water by reverse osmosis,

de-ionization and proprietary process

with USP medical-grade oxygen.

Dayvon was born Jan. 5, 2013, and the family used tap water in his formula, unknowingly giving him a chemical with uncertain health impacts. They have since limited his consumption to bottled water.

Dayvon toddled about Johnston's Greenwich Avenue home last week in his walker, an Elmo pacifier between his chubby cheeks. Johnston's 8-year-old son, Nathan, has been drinking the water, too.

"I protect them with my life, but ... I'm feeding them water that has poison in it," Johnston, 61, said. She and other family members still drink the water, citing financial constraints.

Microtones, bent tones, and hertzes of humming.

There are long nights teeming with characters and their haunted choreographies.

> "I'm struggling," she said.

The punctured page, the paper turned, the trade in waste. The trade in waste, the wasted lives. Scattered everywhere, illegal dumps. But sometimes the saved, the little dogs, the loves. And sometimes I do like to be flying through the rennet forms—the air like curdled milk, because I'm on "a junket" in these clouds with their bounces of movement and their surprises. Streaks streaming from deflected sunlight and all the stories.

TOP OF THE NEWS

The underlying events are wrapped within begin.

> So—begin. **violence:** Survivors say dozens of gunmen on motorbikes have killed more than 100 villagers in a land dispute. **A2**

Exhibit under construction; this gallery is currently closed to the public.

Everything is very steep: harder to pay, harder to walk. It seems now everything is all up hill.

These observations on the everyday contain one grain of truth awash in tap water—but nothing fancy. We hope that it is pure enough.

> "It's difficult to live poor in a well-off area," said Seaton, who makes less than $10,000 annually caring for animals during the summer at Brandywine Picnic Park. "Sometimes, I just can't afford to eat."

If you see ethics, say ethics.

Comprehension passage and required comprehension question.
Test: part 3.

"Betty Olson's diary!" said the well-known literary critic and biographer.
"I have got to get to it before the feminists do."

The great poet has died. I have to give one of many addresses at his
funeral. I lose the address of the big house before I find it. The funeral
is so big it is held in two shifts. Many strange people wander around
the large property. Then (imagine!) a well-known feminist drives up in
a semi-, careening wildly and madly up the road-wide driveway and
smashes directly into the house. There is no doubt she too has died.
People call the police. There is only a recorded announcement on their
machine, and so they never come. Meantime, I never speak.

The stamps (33¢) of Malcolm X had been cancelled by machine. Then
someone took a black marker pen and double cancelled them. Really X'd
them out. "There are several areas of concern, and I will try to outline
them as best I can without giving the prehistory of everything." Yes,
I'm trying to keep on target, but the target keeps moving. Then Ann
called and we talked for an hour—both her parents dying just like that,
"two for the price of one," she said. The snow makes everything cozy.
"Complexity is not a crime, but carry/ it to the point of murkiness/ and
nothing is plain."

•

from the site. How much leaked,
and whether the leak was a crim-
inal act, is at issue.
Environmental groups have

Now that you have read this passage carefully, identify which parts of it
actually happened. Defend your position and develop your ideas fully.

So why did he think that she was producing gibberish
when she was only working a level of language
as if cellular or skims
caught just under the frozen surface
as if changing between ice and water,
changing between clouds types as time blows through them,
the language
one speaks in dreams,
but not in dreams he has had
or maybe does not remember having.

"Sleep is a challenge
to the unity of the subject."

Isn't ANYTHING?

It is.

"Thank you for taking the time to inform me
of your position on this important issue."

PROVERBS

Write with the threads visible.

Insouciant skibbling still needs to have backbone.

No one should say, "You know, I have more tools in my basement than you do." But they are allowed to think it.

Have all your people, have all your voices, talk to each other.

One could have poetry printed on labels for jars of honey. But why only on honey?

A succinct minimalism seems best. Too bad this is not it.

A hole penetrates the page, a pinhole. A little black smudge came onto the page accidentally, un-erasable. Those are the sources. Sorcerers.

There is no "whole" as such. One curlicue, one excessive note, mark, intonation, interpretive or suggestive cadence, one bit of fancy or willfulness, and the "whole" exceeds itself, displaces its ideal state.

All books are therefore of another mind.

MORE ADVICE

The green piping. The green piping is best.

To spin the poles of no and yes, take a deep breath backward.

Let nothing become mannerism.

Do not get into an eating contest with your father!

But forget about implausible exorcisms. Go for the plausible.

It is a loose form. A loose forum. The stakes that high. Were always so.

Knock. Knock forever. Then reach forward and open the door.

What is encrypted here?

What is the shadow of this word?

These pens are inadequate for the perfect scriptorium—and will always be.

Why is the not-yet disclosed so palpable and yet so evanescent?

Wake up, change clocks, download. Uptick.

These pens will only work in the imperfect scriptorium.

Understand that internal translation will never cease.

All poems I write are shadow poems. As in an eclipse, the engulfing reddish pigment of earth's sunsets shadows the orb, displaying it more clearly as a solid, hanging sphere. It is the shock of proof, like mountains on the moon, or the moons of Jupiter. Who traveled from Mt. Olympus to Mt. Oulipos? It wasn't me. Or was it? I was flirty on this question. Did these words come here from the grave vase tube? Or did I write this? Is this female "thing" important? and when? This picking, gleaning, arranging, these tales about the birds and of the snake—what now? For fables have to be made like a plumb line. Coastal Redwoods are so tall they create their own rain. Do they make clouds by assembling nearby air or pierce right through the vaporous air that's already palpable? They pull into their needles high at the tops of the tree the foggy moisture of a coast where mist pulses toward them almost every day. And 83,000 lightening strikes were reported in one stormy 24 hours—by weather researchers in another magnetic country. The meditation about death he read at the funeral never used that word. Every poem writes, rewrites, or reassembles some part of the former history of poetry and yet penetrates that misty float, creating its own rain.

A poetics of the encounter
       finds
              that the domain of the ethical

is also
       the domain
          of the ordinary.

Electric light blue snow at dusk marks the side shapes of structures.
Beauty is true (though is beauty truth?), but what about the
support systems for all this heightening? Timelessness only exists
partially. If at all. He called me up to say that she had died, "in a way
silent, mysterious, difficult to discern." What is this world of such
disappearance that I am in it? At least those hairy lichens like tinsel
on the tree say the air in this forest is still free of impurity. Or so the
docent said. But when we did an Earth Day cleanup in another creek,
we dredged out bottles, cans, pillboxes, softballs and styrofoam. She
had looked so pale and hairless, then well-coiffed. "It's a wig," she said.
Always ready to dot that i with utter honesty. Sign in the ladies room:
"Hurting? God Cares." Can't top that, right? A Dedalean tuft scrolled
overall like a finial, a cherubic decor. As for me, I've made no secret of
it: want deformed words, want bits of alphabet formed into statements
facing a sudden encounter, want to know what is really there, want
chakra phonemes hanging over the page as from a void. . . .

if you want these things then work with work upon work.

All this illegibility was piling up. Well, not illegibility. Each item, each notation is perfectly legible. It's the question of finishing off. Of structure. Of a sense of the whole. These terms are said to indicate "meaning." But I wanted neither, or not in the usual way. I did not want to come to terms.

The stones, the roofs in shadow, the roofs in sunlight, stand draftsman-like, presenting an excitable surface for the difference light makes across the unidirectional plasticity of time. Draftsperson. To shuttle between plein air and the studio as official sites ritualized painterly practices. The elegant set of trees you see in that sketch is nicknamed "the bouquet of painters." It is moveable to any site in any work. Picturesque, it makes a winsome skill set that we can appreciate. The alphabet he used, in contrast, looked like it had been dunked in crankcase oil. It all depends.

Small modulations of difference add up. Translation is the basic human need after getting food and water, sex, shelter, tools (then maybe clothes) and sanitation. All involve a kind of reading from the start. So what did the Cro Magnon and the Neanderthal say to each other. Whatever—it must have been perfectly charming. All that curiosity and touching. Aggression? Insistence? Try-outs of words? Sex for sure. Lust and language: the lust for language. After that—perhaps exchanges of jewelry. Trickery. Challenges. Maybe laughter. And teaching each other to count.

They came in and ripped out our walls, right down to the brick. Amazing to see what lay behind those walls—no insulation, and that was the problem. Amazing to see what is "in" a house. The poise, force, vectors, and counter-thrust do hold, even when, proving a correct prediction by the contractor, there was a serious gap and therefore sag, old bricks subsiding just under the window. Now we are more true. More trued. "When you are building a house, do not leave it rough-hewn, or a cawing crow may settle on it and croak." Yes, croak. That's how the translator put it. Croak. Condensing the bad luck sign in one sound and one event in one fell swoop.

But what would be political outcomes and implications, if they had intended to rip up the house, their project precisely and only to destroy it? Sinks smashed off the walls, broken stair treads, a child's sneaker fallen off and left behind, doors kicked in, shit deliberately left on the floor, everything axed and trashed. Rendered uninhabitable. There are certain realities just like that. Do you or I or anyone know?

PLOT

Is time crystallized inside things? If one could enter things again and find it and re-saturate? It seems against the laws of physics. But then why collect—that rock, that shell to decorate your house?

At least water flows through these pipes and is not cut off by armies. Not betrayed by industry and smart-mouthed by legalese.

The mourning doves sit and fluff out, adjusting themselves comfortably under our outside table, a place that protects them from hawks.

A friend said to a tourist, trying to wise her up, "You know Americans are not that well liked here right now." She wrote him later in an email: "I hope you are dealing with your anger."

And, by the way, "heavenly hurt" does not mean it is a "more soothing" hurt than that which is achieved on earth.

Well, the student said, it was just an educative guess.

What has changed now that we are able to feel this is in fact the 21st century? Is it just those fourteen or sixteen years gone by? Is it that the ecological disaster of humankind changing the face of the earth has gotten faster, greater in scale, more—irreversible? But the Great Plains and animal extinction (Native American depredation, several centuries ago) is fairly irreversible; the desertification of the Sahara (North African depredation, many centuries ago) is so far irreversible; the deforestation of Greece (Classical depredation, back in B.C.E.) has not recovered across the whole arc of Western civilization. The California coast was once so thick with trees—often giant, ancient redwoods—that the Spanish thought San Francisco Bay was just a creek and passed that harbor by. These were later logged to build the city twice, once during the Gold Rush and then after the earthquake and fire. Tar sands now despoil areas of Canada; Fukushima despoils the Pacific Ocean; the abrupt loss of Amazon rain forest is seen from satellite photographs—all this dramatic depredation and disaster has changed the scale, but has it changed the impact long term? Are planets simply there (wherever there is) inevitably to be used up and burnt out? Is the universe fecund as a whole, but then what about us? (A biscuit conditional—is it?) This is the only "us" we know. Blank hard words. Words. These are words. This universe might not count in centuries, might not even count at all. Works and days, and days and works.

We live together—different people, a passel of friends. A generation or two, modulation. Time passes. It's normal. You remember to look around. It is a landscape of slowly changing shapes. A hill erodes. Or there is an avalanche. Some fracking; that's different. People are slightly altered. Some "disappear" and we know (we say we know) what this means. Now I understand why certain people (either with or without meaning to) have their diva moments, the intensities of drama or aggressions so obscured in origin one doesn't understand. Such grifts of shouting. Such bitter earworms. Such calls to conquer. A pain so great it becomes illness. Irreversible images. A collapse in one's core, and the spinning of brutalist concrete to pour into that core. Unspeakable events. It is a mode of claiming a presence in time, along the capricious and callow lines of proud conviction; it is marking the world as with a big dark oily crayon of the thickness of a tribe or of a nation. This deliberately done, in desperate cunning and with hawk-like strategy, to change everything— and sometimes it does. The genetic material of others—lost. Languages— lost. To win, to win and to win—a shell of what there was. At least (someone might say in justification—although to whom we cannot know), "I" and "we" have made a memorable—if often damaging— mark. This, by the way, occasionally in the mode of ultimate rightness or of "cleansing." The destruction of others. Or in the concentrated mode of "taking." Yet we need neither cleansing nor despoiling; we need more replenishing. Of whatever is possible.

But I don't understand. The problem of what has sometimes been called evil and sometimes absolute power is not going to be explained in any way by this riffle of rhetoric. There is no mammal so cruel, none so capable of that deep, exhausting, unconscionable level of destruction motivated by its vicious understanding of its apparent "needs," its curious senses of "profit," or "principle" or "soul."

What are the possibilities? I don't know.

At the same time that one branch of government was making ethnographic recordings of tribal and group songs, rituals, and languages, the Indian schools with their "civilizing," normalizing missions were trying to extirpate these cultural products and their social joys. Then a synoptic eclecticism becomes the rage. Then something else. The fashionista approach to everything. So-called "best practices."

Hence I cannot "speak for" anyone—the subaltern? women? The "educated"? I can speak, period, just out of necessity. What is faking? over-coziness with one's own "manner"? Saying things for the "good" of others? I want to change the tonal possibilities—the ethical possibilities!— but poetry has its own histories and aims that cannot be mechanically excluded. Thus negotiation, thus tolerance and curiosity, thus the overflowing of the poem, the over-layering of the poem, a thin ribbon of potentiality, a little (was that the red one?) thread of hope.

When "the lamenting subject threatens to become arrested in its condition," think of the redwoods. A live redwood that is knocked over will attempt to continue growing via its limbs. If undisturbed, the limbs pointing up will turn into trees in their own right. This is the source of many row groups of trees. Genetically, it's the same tree after each successive cloning process. It can be the same tree, turned into many, over many thousand years. These are closer to sidereal time than we. We breathe the air that they exhale.

The desire for hemiola, a triple rhythm in the space for two, a one-and-a-half, an extra twist, the leap between pulses that cannot simply be suppressed. See light through your ears. Move the boundaries of the possible. Layer bravery. Study authenticity. Do not seek wholeness but further fields of unevenness.

68

The incomparable, the scale off,
the translocated, exiled, awkward and alarmed,
the clatter, the shattering.
the things that do not fit,
these arrive and settle in here.
It is another rebalancing ecology.

Trying for an ultimate, that point of X crossing intensity with fervor and yet beyond those emotions (of excitement, say, or pleasure, or fear, or even awe)—I realize quietly that the ultimate is a filled silence. A silence of matter and languages so rich (yet not turgid), so clear (but not plain), so poised between all and nothing, between poles positive and negative that it could be called both enlightenment and endarkenment. It does not pass in any way through the ego. It happens outside and yet suffuses the thing I sit inside of—self. The incipient has precipitated. And yet the world is ever in motion and does not stop. This moment cannot be—not as such, not permanent, but perhaps it can be reconstituted, opened by chance, stumbled upon. It's probable that the only way to indicate it—I mean enlightenment over and under endarkenment—is not through the full but through the progressively more eroded, more erased, more empty—that nonetheless feels adequate. Adequate to what is. Representation (as such, as we know it) might simply be beside the point. The conventions of tuning, the consonances are simply irrelevant. But one might want to show. To demonstrate. To offer.

> Language pulses
> with all that can be made of it
> along the lines of understanding.
> Vulnerability, said the mite,
> and Yes, said the dot.
> Various tree stuff floats through the air
> on puffs of wind, and lands with little pings.
> The words
> people write, the things they say
> are investments in
> that oddity.

The froth and pleasures of representations—and they are lavish and lovely—somewhat confuse what choices of words might indicate such a filled and silent space. Call this space "and yet." Call it "as such." The dates and days of the week. The works inside those days. Do you feel it sometimes?—a fecund emptiness. Yet it is not about following but accumulation into continuum. The first day's sunset had a purple streak; the second day it was a bowl of orange pink.

At least imagine cryptic outlines of something
for a variety of materials that forward,
poetry porous entity trying continuance
poetry positing but emptying
poetry spontaneous entryway

sang the nightingale wildly
blurting song out
as it often does
at dawn.

Sun spout, wind spot, line of clouds. But I don't want another word about the weather. How about: the downed mid-sized sapling has frozen clods still attached and mingled with the roots in which four or five bulb shoots—early narcissus, though on their side and falling off —were wonderfully firm and greening. Impossible to calculate livid hopes; just try counting only in such conjunctures.

So that "behind the unfolding is another unfolding. So there's this emptying out, or flattening. But it is not an emptying that makes things empty." It is lassitude.

About his carving of individual staffs, made, out of their ethos and poetics, for individual poets to help them on their journeys through their works and their days, Jacob Manu Scott observed: "once you start putting meaning in one little bit of it—you're kind of stuck with it."

We have entered the space of being. We will not live in capitulate-ism. We will resist.

Tentative pipings of spring birds doing little notes, speaking, like me in a dream, dreamy inaccurate Italian. The blue snake is still a-roaming, luminous, deep in the box of the house.

Not another word.

REFERENCES

Newspaper clippings were taken from *The Philadelphia Inquirer, The New York Times,* and the *San Francisco Chronicle* during the last months of 2013 and the first months of 2014, when this work was written. My apologies to journalists whose by-line I lost; my interest was often in the citations they featured, from people speaking about what they knew. As many by-line sources as I could, I noted. My reading of Hesiod was in *Works And Days* as translated by Hugh G. Evelyn-White and published in 1914, one hundred years ago.

1. Was life created

"Opened with two quadruple salchows, the first in combination with a double toe loop, and did seven other triples." From an AP article on Max Aaron, who won the 2012 figure skating crown.

Some part of the end of section 1 is from composer John Adams, probably the words "a sustained resonance."

4. Audio Combine for laptop

"Audio Combine for laptop, toy chimes, music box, ukulele and hand drum." Work by John Bischoff; the description of his instrumentation from the brochure "Other Minds—A festival of unexpected new music" held San Francisco Jazz Center, 2014.

"African grey parrot, blue parrotlet, muted violin, trumpet, stone/bowl of water, Buchia Lighting and digital recording." Work by Wendy Reid, same festival.

"Mobile phones, coins, foil gum wrappers, keys, heavy jewelry, belt buckles, hair clips, and metal in clothing including buttons, snaps, and underwire bras an set off the detector, so think before you get dressed." (Brochure, TSA tips for traveling)

5. So what if I am having

"the borderline between a pile of refuse and an artwork was never more than obscure." Gwendolyn Webster, Menil Catalogue on Kurt Schwitters.

"movement, action, gesture and solidified ephemera." Christine Froula from "Modernity, Drafts, Genetic Criticism" in Yale French Studies 113.

Biscuit conditionals courtesy of linguist Muffy Siegel, Temple University.

"We spin around in the night and are consumed by fire." Guy Debord, his film title from the Medieval palindrome "*In girum imus nocte et consumimur igni.*"

7. Before I departed

Rangitoto—a distinctive, low-slung symmetrical volcanic island that erupted in historical time, in Hauraki Gulf, near Auckland, New Zealand.

8. He died . . .

The title *Standing in Another Man's Grave* is Ian Rankin's, a book from 2012.

9. Starry False Solomon's Seal

Report on the meeting of the American Astronomical Society by Seth Borenstein for the Associated Press.

Citations from Ludwig Wittgenstein, *Tractatus Logico-Philosophicus.* Trans. C.K. Ogden. New York: Harcourt, Brace & Company, Inc., 1922.

12 and 18. But St. Lucy's

Nerve gas references to the "accidental" killing of 6000 sheep grazing 45 miles away with chemical agents blown from the Dugway Proving Grounds in Utah, USA, showing that the Army was testing chemical and biological weapons —a revelation at the time (1968), both for the facts and for the rhetorics of justification and astonishment. Headline: "Army's Nerve Gas Feared in Denver." *The New York Times,* August 18, 1968.

14. Speaking from

The whirlwind book—seen on Silk Road Exhibit, British Museum, 2004. The allusion to the poet is to Louis Zukofsky, who insisted he was cleaning his desk in a section of "A"-12.

15. Please don't wish

"Please, don't wish people a Happy Yom Kippur; it's not a happy holiday." An etiquette statement from www.jwfaq.org/express.htm

Carolyn Lochhead of the San Francisco Chronicle with its series (March 24, 2014) of the impact on California of long-term agricultural practices combined with severe drought.

18. A tilt, a modulation

The advice column implied question and answer from <tellme@washpost. com>

The nightingale and the hawk from Hesiod, ll. 202–211

20. Are these identical units

A now untraceable riff on Robert Creeley's remark, famously cited by Charles Olson in "Projective Verse."

Citation from the obituary of Franklin McCain, one of the Greensboro Four who occupied the segregated lunch counter at Woolworth's in 1960 in protest. Obituary written by Emery P. Dalesio, Associated Press.

23. If we all became radioactive

Peter Parker, bitten by a "radioactive spider," became Spider-Man®.

26. X is back from

Article in *The Philadelphia Inquirer,* by-lines John Heilprin and Barbara Surk, Associated Press. Citation about barrel bombs from Trudy Rubin, *The Philadelphia Inquirer.*

28. He has power cords snaking

The visual work of Amze Emmons.

Article about poverty in West Chester, PA is by Alfred Lubrano, *The Philadelphia Inquirer,* December 18, 2013. Also cited in Sections 23 and 41.

29. Grasses for sheep

This is a gloss on three words in my "For the Etruscans": "the almost thrilling ambition to write a great, encyclopedic, holistic work, an ambition to get everything in, inclusive, reflexive, monumental." From *The Pink Guitar: Writing as Feminist Practice*.

32. Who are we

Notes on the diffusion of languages from Beringia, the temporary land mass in the Bering Strait, populated about 15,000 years before today, as postulated by John F. Hoffecker, University of Colorado. *The New York Times*, March 13, 2014 by Nicholas Wade. This interpretation is in debate.

33. Starry lake of sky

The exegete transformed by the practice of exegesis is paraphrased from Michael Fishbane, *The Exegetical Imagination: On Jewish Thought and Theology*. Harvard UP 1998, 110.

34. A harmonious accord

A perfume advertisement by Dior in US Airways Duty-Free Shopping Catalogue.

35 and elsewhere. Dying through the spring

Citations and other absorbed words describing clouds are taken from an old U.S. Government document revised 5-1-1956 called "Definitions and Descriptions of the Forms of Clouds." Personal copy.

42. Even if we return

Respectively Jackson Mac Low and Clarence Blau.

43. If you obey my voice

The stipulations of the God of the Covenant in Exodus 25–28, *passim*.

Article on yarnbombing by Rita Giordano, *The Philadelphia Inquirer*, Feb. 9, 2014.

"A research team led by Dr. John Stamatoyannopoulos, University of Washington, has discovered a second code hidden in DNA. This second code contains information that changes how scientists read the instructions contained in DNA and interpret mutations to make sense of health and disease.

"Since the genetic code was deciphered in the 1960s, scientists have assumed that it was used exclusively to write information about proteins. UW scientists were stunned to discover that genomes use the genetic code to write two separate languages. One describes how proteins are made, and the other instructs the cell on how genes are controlled. One language is written on top of the other, which is why the second language remained hidden for so long."

The work is part of the Encyclopedia of DNA Elements Project, also known as ENCODE. The National Human Genome Research Institute funded the multi-year, international effort. ENCODE aims to discover where and how the directions for biological functions are stored in the human genome. From *The New York Times*, probably, via *Science*.

45. His passport photo

The passport photo of Walter Benjamin.

Article on lung transplants by Sandy Bauers, *The Philadelphia Inquirer*, Feb. 5, 2014.

51. Why do the extremities

"This is the only way to achieve the floating or uncertain nature of things." The citation is from a feature article by David Patrick Stearns about the German composer Wolfgang Rihm, *The Philadelphia Inquirer*, December 20, 2013.

53. You're holding in your hand

This section is a verbatim citation of the label from a Penta™ ultra-purified water bottle.

Citation from the article by Angelo Fichera, about the contaminating industrial spill into the water supply in West Virginia, *The Philadelphia Inquirer*, Feb. 9, 2014.

55. Comprehension passage

"Complexity is not a crime, but carry/ it to the point of murkiness / and nothing is plain." Marianne Moore, of course, "In the Days of Prismatic Color." There is also a version that places the line break inside the word "murki- / ness." *The Complete Poems of Marianne Moore*. New York: The Macmillan Company/The Viking Press, 1981.

56. So why did he think

Letter to his constituents in PA-182 (Philadelphia County) by Rep. Brian Sims.

59. What is encrypted here

With thanks to Divya Victor, who presented my words back to me.

60. All poems I write

Article on the snowy owl and other severely disrupted patterns of fauna in the current environmental crisis is by Jacqueline L. Urgo, *The Philadelphia Inquirer,* December 22, 2013.

61. A poetics of the encounter

This statement is taken, slightly modified, from Peter Nicholls, "Oppen: Of Being Ethical," *The Objectivist Nexus: Essays in Cultural Poetics,* ed. Rachel Blau DuPlessis and Peter Quartermain, Tuscaloosa: The University of Alabama Press, 1999, 251. Nicholls is paraphrasing Emmanuel Levinas.

62. Electric light blue

The last line is from Hesiod, trans. Evelyn-White, ll. 381–382.

63. All this illegibility

The crow from Hesiod, Evelyn-White, ll. 746–747.

68. What are the possibilities

"The lamenting subject threatens to become arrested in its condition" is Theodor Adorno, *Minima Moralia: Reflections from Damaged Life* (1951). Trans. E.F.N. Jephcott. Verso, 2006, 16.

72. Sun Spout

The first citation is from Holly Bittner, personal communication. The second from Maori wood carver / artist Jacob Manu Scott, in his speech at the 2011 Maori ceremonial investiture of Ian Wedde as New Zealand (term) poet laureate (2011–13).

About the Author

A 2002 Pew Fellow in the Arts, and a recipient of poetry fellowships from Djerassi and The Rockefeller Foundation (Bellagio), Rachel Blau DuPlessis is the author of the critically acclaimed long poem *Drafts* (1986-2012) in 114 cantos. *Days and Works* is one of her "interstitial" books, a group that includes *Interstices* (Subpress, 2014), *Graphic Novella* (Xexoxial Editions, 2015), the collage-poem *Numbers* (forthcoming from Materialist Press), and *Eurydics* (forthcoming from Further Other Book Works). DuPlessis has written a trilogy of critical essays on gender and poetics: *The Pink Guitar, Blue Studios* and *Purple Passages,* and several other critical books, as well as editing *The Selected Letters of George Oppen* (1990). She has embarked on a 21st–century long poem, called *Traces*.

AHSAHTA PRESS

NEW SERIES

AHSAHTA PRESS

SAWTOOTH POETRY PRIZE SERIES

2002: Aaron McCollough, *Welkin* (Brenda Hillman, judge)

2003: Graham Foust, *Leave the Room to Itself* (Joe Wenderoth, judge)

2004: Noah Eli Gordon, *The Area of Sound Called the Subtone* (Claudia Rankine, judge)

2005: Karla Kelsey, *Knowledge, Forms, The Aviary* (Carolyn Forché, judge)

2006: Paige Ackerson-Kiely, *In No One's Land* (D. A. Powell, judge)

2007: Rusty Morrison, *the true keeps calm biding its story* (Peter Gizzi, judge)

2008: Barbara Maloutas, *the whole Marie* (C. D. Wright, judge)

2009: Julie Carr, *100 Notes on Violence* (Rae Armantrout, judge)

2010: James Meetze, *Dayglo* (Terrance Hayes, judge)

2011: Karen Rigby, *Chinoiserie* (Paul Hoover, judge)

2012: T. Zachary Cotler, *Sonnets to the Humans* (Heather McHugh, judge)

2013: David Bartone, *Practice on Mountains* (Dan Beachy-Quick, judge)

2014: Aaron Apps, *Dear Herculine* (Mei-mei Berssenbrugge, judge)

2015: Vincent Toro, *Stereo. Island. Mosaic.* (Ed Roberson, judge)

2016: Jennifer Nelson, *Civilization Makes Me Lonely* (Anne Boyer, judge)

This book is set in Apollo MT and Helvetica Neue type
by Ahsahta Press at Boise State University.
Cover design by Quemadura.
Book design by Janet Holmes.

AHSAHTA PRESS

2017

JANET HOLMES, DIRECTOR

PATRICIA BOWEN, *intern*

SAM CAMPBELL

KATHRYN JENSEN

COLIN JOHNSON

DAN LAU

MATT NAPLES